Sensational Settings

A Quick Guide to Writing Well

P.S. Wells

Pegwood Publishing

Title: How to Shape Sensational Settings

By P.S. Wells

Subjects: 1. Authorship Reference (Books)

2. Writing Skill Reference (Books)

3. Creativity (Books)

Key Words: How to write, character, character-driven story, creativity, fiction writing, write story, write fiction

ISBN ebook: 979-8-9921044-0-0

ISBN paperback: 979-8-9921044-1-7

Published by Pegwood Publishing

Roanoke IN 46783

Contents

Chapter One

On Your Mark, Get Set, Write

B efore you begin writing, save time and effort by knowing these three things.

1. What is your idea?

2. Who is your audience?

3. How does your idea, message, or story benefit your audience?

4. What is the best method to share your idea to your particular audience?

Every project begins with an idea.

First, decide what is the story or message, lesson or insight you want to share?

Hone the idea down to a laser point. The tighter the focus the better you stay on target. The tighter the message the easier for your reader to follow where you take them.

Do not be intimidated to find others have written on the same topic. You have your own slant, your own experience, your own insight which is unique to you. There is always room in the market for fresh ways of thinking on a familiar topic. Your voice will be different from other authors.

Put considerable thought into how you will present your idea in a unique fashion.

What is your idea?

Second, you have an idea, message, or story you want to share. The question is, who do you want to share your message with?

Before you begin, clarify exactly who you are speaking to. This is as important as dialing a specific number when you make a phone call.

No project – outside God's Word – is for everyone. Who is your target audience? Who is interested in receiving your message?

Age, education level, ethnicity, faith, gender, hobbies, interests, and profession are among the considerations when you define your audience. Academics, artists, and athletes each have unique jargon and terminology as do zoning specialists, zoologists, and zoo keepers. Bestselling author, Jerry Jenkins, pictured his mother sitting across the desk as he wrote his novels. She represented the audience he had in mind for the stories he told.

How specific can you be when you describe your audience?

· *The Ten Best Decisions A Single Mom Can Make* is practical help and tangible tips for solo parents ages 24 to 45, eager to create a healthy and successful family.

· *Slavery in the Land of the Free* informs intermediate and high school students about human trafficking in the United States.

· Geared for four to eight-year-olds, *The Girl Who Wore Freedom* is the true story of five-year-old Dany who was given Lifesavers and liberty on D-Day.

Writing to children is completely different from communicating with teens which differs from sharing with adults. Generally speaking, the vocabulary that appeals to women is not the same as the descriptions that resonate with men. While the words in a toddler's board book are chosen as carefully as the text for a novel, the volume is exceedingly fewer. Knowing your audience guides your vocabulary level and the length of your project in the same way you craft a conversation with an industry professional far differently than you prepare to talk with a child.

Third, how does your idea, message, or story benefit your audience? Why would your reader trade their hard-earned funds to purchase your project? Why would someone invest their limited time to read your writing?

In other words, what take-home value do you provide?

Types of take-home value writers offer include

- entertainment

- education

- guidance

- humor

- how-to instruction

- inspiration

- information

When you pen a project to be viewed and consumed by others, you create an exchange. You expect your audience to read your writing. Your audience expects you will make the experience of reading your work worthwhile. To keep your end of the agreement, clarify the benefit you plan to provide. Purposefully and generously give your audience abundant take-home value.

Fourth, once you know your audience and the take-home value you will provide to that audience, it's time to decide on the best vehicle to convey your message. There are myriad ways for a writer to communicate including

apps
articles
books
children's books
curriculum
greeting cards
novel
screenplay

song

web content

As writers, we have myriad formats to connect with readers. When you know your target audience, and the take-home value you want to deliver, then consider what format will be the most effective to share your message. You have plenty of options.

If you plan to write a book or want to improve a story, place the tale in a sensational setting. Stories happen in a place and that place is the setting.

Chapter Two

Setting Is

You have a story to share, a message to tell through writing. There are foundational aspects to writing well including a well-crafted setting.

Essentials for a powerful story are

    1. a character the reader cares about

    2. a very great life-changing, world-impacting need the character must achieve

    3. a great obstacle between the character we care about and the character's life-changing, world-impacting need

Critical elements for a compelling, memorable story that works include

- Pivotal Plots

- Memorable Characters

- Sensational Settings

- Dynamic Dialog

- Point of View

Stories happen in a place and that place is the setting.
Setting comprises a story's

- Time

- Place

- Surroundings

- Mood

- Cultural nuances

- Historical period

- A backdrop for a story

- Setting can be the story

Settings come in four personalities.
The personalities types of setting are

- Passive

- Active

- Like a Character

- Is the Story

A story can travel to encompass several or all of the types of settings. The tale can move in no particular order from a passive background to an active backdrop, from functioning like a character to being the focus of the story.

In each setting where your story takes place, describe to your reader what is unusual. Skip telling the reader what is typical, common, or ordinary. Focus on what is atypical, what the reader may not know or otherwise notice.

Use the five senses to share with the reader the smell and taste of the setting. What does the setting sound like, feel like, and look like?

A writer has one job to do and that is to elicit an emotional response in the reader. How can you use setting to elicit emotion from your reader?

Chapter Three

Passive Setting

A passive setting happens when the background is so ordinary as to be nearly invisible.

Here's an example from my story, *Is That All*.

*Immediately **upon giving birth** to her fifth child, **Nelma's** arms were empty. The **hospital staff** whisked away the baby before she could see him.*

"I want to see my son," Nelma insisted.

*"You need to understand, there are problems with the baby." The **doctor** explained that perhaps Nelma and **her husband** should consider an institution for their newborn.*

"I want to see my son," Nelma repeated.

*So the new bundle of babe was brought and placed in his mother's arms. Nelma smelled the sweet new baby smell of him; she cooed to the little boy and cradled him to her heart. Then, ever so carefully, she unwrapped **his blanket**. **<u>There lay her infant, born without legs, his hands and arms not fully developed.</u>** Nelma took it all in, caressed his soft new skin, and smiled into his trusting eyes.*

"Oh," she said softly, "is that all?"

In this story, the hospital is a passive setting because, typically, readers are familiar with medical facilities. From personal experience or television and film, readers know how hospitals function, look, and smell. Penning *Is That All*, I did not need to describe what doctors, nursing staff, moms, dads, and babies look like. We are familiar with the birth process, baby blankets, and the general appearance of a newborn.

To describe these aspects of the story would merely bog down the pace and bore the reader into a coma. Additionally, these cast members are not *this* story.

While readers know what babies generally look and act like, I described *this* baby because this child's unique, out-of-the-ordinary appearance *is* the story. *There lay her infant, born without legs, his hands and arms not fully developed.*

When writing the setting for your story, allow the common staging to passively blend nearly invisible into the background. Short descriptions place your reader with your characters in a familiar background that frames the story.

- Walking in the forest

- Sitting in the pew, second row piano side

- Aboard the commercial flight

- Pacing in the Oval Office

- Saddling the horse

- From the passenger seat of the car

- During dinner

- At her desk

- In the theater

- On the beach

- Talking over brunch

- Scanning the crowd

- Paris that year

- Beside the waterfall

- Under the table

- Working in the lab

- The caravan traveled west

- A sailor delivered the commander's meal from the galley as Gennett reviewed his orders on the bridge.

Powerful drama can happen in the most undramatic places. Passive or familiar settings require less description and provide contrast between the ordinary background and the unusual conflict that makes the story.

Trust your reader to know the common bits of the background so you can focus on the uncommon elements that create story.

As your story unfolds, use setting to tell the reader *when* and *where* they are, and how the surroundings influence character, dialog, and plot.

Chapter Four

Active Setting

A ctive settings create an environment that contributes to the story. For instance,

- *The Scarlet Pimpernel* is set in Paris during the French Revolution. The political climate, modes of travel, communication, societal categories, and madame guillotine had powerful influences on the story.

- The film, *Crocodile Dundee,* loosely based on Rod Ansel whose story is told in *Outback Heart* by Joanne Van Os has an active setting in the Australian Outback complete with – well – crocodiles.

- *Secrecy Order*, takes place in a kibbutz. Placed deep in Israel's Negev desert, the communal living isolates our hero in proximity to smugglers of illegal arms.

Following their long-legged host, Marc eyed their surroundings. They were on a hillside overshadowed by higher hills fringing a canyon. Below, the rocky terrain flowed into a wide, dry wadi bed. Two donkeys, a camel, a rust-fringed Mitsubishi truck, and a dusty jeep were parked in the shadow of the hill they were descending. The threesome followed a shallow horizontal groove carved into the thirsty hillside. Gradually angling down, the man-made depression disappeared under the base of a rock-lined well.

Perched on the edge of the well, Adi tossed a bucket into the water below. Hand over hand, he pulled the rope that brought the filled container back to the top. Balancing the bucket on the rim, he removed the fabric tied about his head. He strained the water through his scarf into the trough of hewn rock that sat beside the well. Three times he repeated this process. With a wave of his hand, he indicated they should help themselves.

After washing, Marc and Lei climbed into the dusty jeep and Adi steered the vehicle along cliff edges, plunged into deep dry wadi beds, and climbed steep passes. The few times Adi used the brakes, they piercingly squealed their protest at being coaxed to work.

At last, an oasis appeared in the desert and the vehicle sped toward this place. As they drove, the desert gave way to acres of carefully maintained orchards, gardens tented under white plastic, and pasture animals grazing among sparse crops of wild grasses. Adi parked the jeep beside a cluster of well-kept buildings.

"Where are we?" Lei's legs were wobbly after the wild ride. Before Marc could offer, Adi took her hand to steady the girl as she climbed from the jeep.

Their host gave a grand sweep with his free hand. "This is my home, my kibbutz."

- In *Homeless for the Holidays,* the Arctic Artie's bathroom actively places our hero, Jack Baker, in a contemporary American fast-food restaurant where employees make minimum wage and occasionally wear the company's mascot costume.

Jack looked ridiculous in the Arctic Artie's penguin mascot costume. He resembled an oversized, out-of-place, non-flight bird.

As if to confirm his thoughts, a tough looking guy emerged from the bathroom stall and smirked. Locking eyes with Jack, the cocky guy washed his hands, dried them on a paper towel, and tucked the used, wet towel into Jack's white penguin shirt. The man tweaked Jack's plastic penguin beak and left.

The humiliating experience left a bitter taste in his mouth. Standing in a fast-food restaurant bathroom, making minimum wage, dressed like a penguin was a far cry from the VP office he had worked hard for, deserved, and pridefully occupied.

Whether using a passive or active setting, describe for the reader what is unusual. A fast-food restaurant is familiar to the reader, but not an Arctic Artie penguin costume. Paris in the 1700s is different from any other large city of the period when the setting includes the haunting sound of the guillotine.

Chekov's gun is the Russian author's reference to active setting. "One must never place a loaded rifle on the stage if it isn't going to go off. It's wrong to make promises you don't mean to keep." In *Chasing*

Sunrise, our hero puts on equipment to scuba dive. For the most part, readers know what a wet suit looks like. Mentioning Michael's dive knife worked in the beginning of the novel because he uses it in a dramatic scene toward the end. If the dive knife is never used in the story, then it should not be noted in the description of the setting.

When writing setting, include time, place, surroundings, mood, and cultural nuances necessary to the story. Edit out any background that does not contribute.

Chapter Five

Setting as a Character

C haracters in a story think, feel, and act. When a setting acts on the story, the setting takes on a character-like role. A setting can be as three-dimensional as a character.

- The Atlantic Ocean is a force to contend with for the nineteenth century whaling ship, Pequod, in *Moby Dick*.

- Wonderland is a perpetual curiosity Alice must navigate in Louis Carroll's *Alice's Adventures in Wonderland*.

- The High Uintas Wilderness is a wildly unforgiving force to contend with in Charles Martin's disaster romance, *The Mountain Between Us*.

Settings that function like a character exhibit moods, reactions, and responses. For instance, the novel *Chasing Sunrise* takes place mostly on the Caribbean island of St. Croix. From manchineel trees to hurricanes, the setting continually interacts with the characters, often forcing our hero to decide between two bad choices.

As three-dimensional as a character, St. Croix is

- Moody. Warmer temperatures dictate clothing, foods, and activities.

- Reacting. Air pressure, temperature, wind, and the movement of the surrounding sea determine availability of fresh water and the frequency of destructive hurricanes.

- Limited. There are only two cities on St. Croix, no freeways, and a single airport with few flights.

- Contained. As an island, there is a clear beginning and end to the area. Depending on weather, distance, and convenience, the island is isolated from resources.

- Responding. Immediately off-shore is the mile-deep wall, and environmental conditions for sea life including coral reefs and an abundance of conch. On shore, the island is one of the few places nurturing the poisonous manchineel tree.

"Manchineel are usually found near the beach," Jerry intoned. "An attractive tree with shade and apples, but they are very dangerous."

"Poisonous?"

"Deadly to everyone except a species of land crab."

Michael thought about the intrepid little crab holed up in the tree stump.

"The fruit is fatal if eaten," Jerry continued. "Columbus discovered the danger after several of his men died."

Michael examined the damage the sap caused to his hand. "If it's so dangerous, why not get rid of the tree?"

"That's just as dangerous." Jerry shook his head. "Maybe more. The tree and its parts contain strong toxins. Standing beneath the tree during rain may cause blistering. Cutting the tree gets the poisonous sap everywhere. Burning the tree causes blindness if the smoke reaches the eyes. Inhaling the smoke blisters the nose, mouth, and respiratory system."

"Flippin' nuisance," Michael groused.

The islanders call themselves Cruzans and speak a lyrical Creole dialect consisting of English with heavy influences of Portuguese, French, Danish, and Dutch.

Having been owned by six different cultures, St. Croix reflects the styles and customs of their history from the remnants of 200 sugar plantations to the calypso drums and dancing mocko jumbies.

The steel drums beat an intoxicating rhythm and four mocko jumbies made their long-legged entrance. Dressed entirely in white, each wore a wide-brimmed hat over a masked face. Below a flowing blouse, loose cotton pants extended for yards from the dancer's waist to the floor. Balancing on stilts ten feet high, the mysterious entertainers gamboled among the tables.

"They look like the Ku Klux Klan on stilts," Bryce observed.

"Mocko jumbies represent a spiritual, ancient African art form," Elise explained. "They are an icon of Virgin Island culture."

19

Towering above their audience, the limber mocko jumbies expertly spun, skipped, and swayed to the irresistible beat of the calypso music. Like a frolicking daddy-long-legs, one of the troupe circled their table.

Where can you place your story so that the backdrop is so interactive that the setting is as three-dimensional as a character?

Chapter Six

Setting is the Story

On July 6, 1944, 1000 freshly minted soldiers boarded the Louisville & Nashville Railroad in Indianapolis bound for the south. From there they would be sent to the European theater of World War II. Hours later, in Campbell County, Tennessee, the engine, tender, and four passenger cars careened over the side of the Jellico Narrows. Plunging down the 50-foot gorge and into the Clear River, the 418 Engine crashed into a massive boulder.

Setting is where your story takes place.

Setting *is* the story in books like *The Perfect Storm*, *The Day The World Came To Town*, and *She Jumped the Tracks*.

- A creative nonfiction that was made into a movie, *The Perfect Storm* by Sebastian Junger follows the 1991 perfect storm that ravaged North America from October 28 through November 4, 1991. The story follows the ferocity of the weather on boats, their crew, rescue personnel, and their families.

- Jim LeFede's *The Day The World Came To Town* is the story of Gander, Newfoundland on 9-11 when the closing of U.S. airspace forced 38 jetliners bound for the United States to land at Gander International Airport in Canada. LeFede follows how a small town with a population of 10,300 responds to the unexpected arrival of 7,000 guests, many of whom do not speak English and are all in various stages of feeling confused, hungry, frightened, and angry.

- Similarly, *She Jumped The Tracks* by John P. Ascher recounts the largest troop train wreck in the United States. Hundreds of Campbell County residents flocked to the scene to help. They made the first rescues using block and tackle slings to hoist the wounded up the side of the gorge to the road. It often took up to ten men to hoist a body up to the road. Some brought welding torches to free the trapped soldiers. In all 34 men died and 75 were injured. Some survivors went on to fight in North Africa. The wreck left scars on the soldiers, their families, and touched the lives of everyone in Jellico for generations.

At the place in Clear River where the locomotive came to rest is a plaque. In the town square is a memorial with the names of the soldiers who perished in the crash. Adjacent to the hardware store is a home-made museum filled with accounts, news, photos, and memorabilia about the train, the wreck, and the important people whose lives were changed on that fateful day.

The welcome mat is out for those who come to remember, to grieve, and to try to understand. My first visit to Jellico was like a pilgrimage. As I studied the photos and newspaper stories, the elderly gentleman who runs the hardware store approached.

"Do you know someone who was on the train?"

"My grandfather."

He nodded, understanding.

"How often do people come to your museum?"

"Every week." He hitched the strap on his overalls. "People come who were on the train. Their families come. They have questions."

There are four types of settings: passive, active, functions like a character, and when setting *is* the story. In my book, *Unnatural Cause,* our sidekick describes her visit to the historic site in Jellico.

The people of the tiny town of Jellico are the keepers of the flame. They understand their setting is the story. Within minutes of my arrival, the town's librarian joined us as well as a photographer from the newspaper who took my photo. The librarian provided a packet of information, and a history DVD. He introduced me to his mother, now a great-grandmother, whose husband had been the teen who watched the train each evening travel the narrows, and who roused the town to rescue the injured and house the survivors.

Authors Sebastian Junger, Jim LeFede, and John P. Ascher wrote books where setting *is* the story.

What stories have you read that center on the setting? Are you writing a story where setting is the theme?

Chapter Seven

Enhance the Setting

S etting is where your story takes place. Settings come in four types: passive, active, functions like a character, and when setting *is* the story.

Setting is

- Time

- Place

- Surroundings

- Mood

- Cultural nuances

- Historical period

- A backdrop for a story

Placing your story in San Francisco? *Mama's Bank Account* is filled *with* sweet family connections and Old Country traditions, a completely different setting than the City by the Bay experienced by Sam Spade in Dashiell Hammett's *Maltese Falcon*. San Francisco for Mama and her family is a place of honest work, a male cat named Elizabeth, visiting authors, and seeing her children come of age. San Francisco is much darker for the gumshoe who lurks in shady hotel rooms, betrayed by a mysterious woman, and given a package by a dying sea captain while he seeks to solve the murder of his partner.

Wherever a story is placed, a writer sets the tone and mood by what is included and what is left out of the setting. Images of a high-performance race track, the serene canals in Venice, a country inn in Vermont, a castle in England, a kibbutz in Israel's desert, and a French child kissing the cheek of a World War II soldier each present a unique background, time frame, mood, and cultural nuances.

Setting is a playground for foreshadowing. Sunny weather reflects peace, resolution, promise, and hope. Inclement forecasts predict bad news, heartbreak, challenges, and difficulties.

- In *Chasing Sunrise*, as Hurricane Hugo bears down on the island, the antagonist becomes a stronger threat, and the stakes rise for our hero, Michael Northington, and those he cares about.

- "The leaves fell early that year," described Hemingway in *A Farewell to Arms*.

- Dorothy sings *Somewhere Over the Rainbow* just before the tornado whisks her away in *The Wizard of Oz*

A setting where common actions go awry, wardrobes malfunction, and routines are interrupted alert readers that something is brewing.

- The parachute doesn't open during a HALO jump in *Chasing Sunrise*.

- While in the shower, the wife of an astronaut nearly loses her wedding ring down the drain in *Apollo 13*.

- In *The Patent*, as the FBI makes a plan to stop America's enemies from stealing the nation's best designs, the boss misses his target when he tosses his coffee cup onto the trash.

Incorporated into setting, color symbolism effectively adds layers of mood and nuance.

Blue and orange are neutral in their symbolism
Black indicates death
Red points to violence and pending bloodshed
Green is for new life
White shows life
Gold represents wealth
Purple signifies royalty
Pink is indicative of femininity
Yellow means bright, summer, hope
Brown symbolizes earthiness (Think Farmer Brown)

The Lone Ranger is dressed in white and rides a white charger, assuring viewers he is the good guy. At the Royal English Court, everyone is in pastel colors except Paul Chauvelin who is entirely in black in the made-for-TV *Scarlet Pimpernel*.

What do the colors of the dresses of Disney princesses say about them?

Use setting to touch the emotions of your reader.

- Take your character through a cemetery, near a ravine, by rushing water, across a busy highway.

- Give a view of a peaceful beach, a baby nursery, or the cheering crowd at the end of an athletic event.

- Have things in your setting malfunction from a non-working phone to the sudden flat tire, the delayed commuter train, and the grid that loses power.

- Insert into your setting a cat that streaks across the path, a legend, an eclipse, a glimpse the character talks themselves out of thinking they saw.

Weather, odors, music, art, food, customs, routines, holiday traditions, and animals are all aspects you can craft into your setting to bring a sense of time, place, and mood.

When struggling to make your writing work, change the setting so the story could not happen anywhere else.

Chapter Eight

Use Setting to Show

U se setting to show the reader where and when the story is without being on the nose in the description.

In *Rediscovering Your Happily Ever After*, one chapter begins this way:

Winter reigned outdoors and inside my heart as the funeral party left the gravesite. Though it was not a Sunday, this collection of life-long music lovers assembled at a country church where the doors stood open and light from inside spilled onto the snow. Wet and cold, we stomped slush from our shoes and were ushered to a seat in the heated fellowship hall where tables were set, and people I didn't know fed me a hot, home-cooked meal of fried chicken, green bean casserole, and mashed potatoes along with all the lemonade I could drink.

From this setting the reader knows

- someone has died

- it's the day of the funeral

- they are in a small town

- the church is warm and welcoming

- outdoors is snowy and cold

- the menu indicates the Midwest

From a novel in the Marc Wayne adventure series comes this description.

She surveyed her closet, settling on a calf-length floral skirt, peasant blouse, and Birkenstocks. She added a puka shell necklace, hoop earrings, and combed her shoulder-length black hair before letting it hang free.

From the fridge, Lucy selected a V-8 and popped open the can as she kicked the door closed with her foot. Tearing a sheet off the magnet-backed calendar on the refrigerator door, the new date glared back at her. April 30. Of course.

Lucy turned her back on the anniversary date, grabbed her keys and macramé purse off the kitchen table, and headed out the door.

This setting tells the reader:

- The time is the late 70s or early 80s based on the clothing and hairstyle

- Lucy is mindful of her health. A V-8 instead of a donut in the morning is a telling choice

- The calendar is on her fridge, not on a cellphone or Apple watch, reinforcing the timeframe

- April 30 is a significant day, but not in a good way

Placing the character in unusual settings, the reader learns important information about personality and motivation through the ways the character responds. In *Chasing Sunrise,* What do you learn about Michael from his responses to a HALO jump?

At 12,000 feet they slammed onto the top of a cloud. From below these sky residents looked like friendly cotton balls and the rounded raindrops from an island rain felt refreshing. Crashing onto their pointy tops from above at 125 miles an hour stung like dropping onto a bed of nails, and despite his waterproof suit, Michael's skin was quickly damp. In the foggy turbulence, Michael struggled to maintain his position in the circle. Holding his bearing was vital to avoid a fatal collision with another team member.

In the dense cloud, he felt cold, disoriented, and alone. Staring below, he waited impatiently for the lights of the world to reappear. In the dark abyss of clouds, Michael checked his glowing altimeter again. The circling hand whirled toward zero. Fear jolted through his body. Instinctively his hand reached to pull his chute. Then he caught himself. The altimeter only went to 13,000. When he jumped from 26,000 feet, he had to remember that the altimeter must make two rounds from 13,000 to zero. This was merely the halfway mark. He fought panic and the fear of hitting the earth like a bug on a windshield.

If you find the story is not working, make the story so it could not happen in any other setting.

If the story is still not working, change the point of view. Write the story from the POV of the character who has the most to lose. For instance, *The Slave Across the Street* is the true story of an upscale Detroit teenager who was trafficked for two years. Two write from the POV of the local police or even the POV of the trafficker is an option. But writing from the view of the girl who was trafficked changes the setting to add tension and suspense.

Writing about Super Bowl XXXII becomes compelling when told from the POV of Bronco Terrell Davis. When the coach told the MVP to run a play, Davis replied that he had lost his sight due to the onset of a migraine. The Super Bowl championship depended on Davis running the play truly blind.

How can you weave the unusual into the description of the setting to show, rather than tell, the reader important information vital to the story?

Chapter Nine

Set Up Setting

Writers come in many types. Traditionally, authors work mostly as outliners, plotters, or plungers, and hybrids of these styles. While I lean to plunger, each project has its own requirements. Stories created in a historical timeline require careful planning which looks a lot like an outline.

Outliner

JK Rowling penned an outline for the fifth Harry Potter novel, *Order of the Phoenix*, on a common piece of notebook paper. Laying the page horizontal, she created a grid with the months of the school year on the left, and the plot points and significant characters listed along the top. When she had filled in the intersecting squares, Rowling knew what needed to happen in each chapter.

Inspired by JK Rowling's masterful Harry Potter series that included separate books that, put together, provided an even larger epic, Lydia Sherrer sketched a plan for Love, Lies, and Hocus Pocus. Each book in the series is a complete adventure for Lily Singer, Sebastian, and Sir Edgar Allen Kipling. When put together, the series tells a larger, overarching story. Each book in the series is a significant contribution to a books-long epic.

Other authors who wrote their books this way include

- JRR Tolkien's *Lord of the Rings*

- CS Lewis' Narnia series

- Louis L'amour's series about the Sackett family

Plotter

Bill Myers, whose books and films sold more than eight million copies and won more than 60 national and international awards, knows where his story will go from beginning to end before he puts words on his manuscript. The author of numerous series for kids, teens, and adults, likes to use the bubble diagram technique. He described writing a seed idea onto a yellow legal pad and circling the idea. From there, Bill creates a bubble diagram, listing a variety of *what next* possibilities, followed by another level of potential plot points, and then another and another until the legal pad is filled.

With a highlighter, Myers reviews the original idea and marks the best next event in each sequence. With this method, he maps the entirety of the story. His writing process involves following the highlighted trail on the legal pad from chapter one until 'The End.'

Plunger

My tendency is to be a plunger. *Chasing Sunrise* began as a scene that hung around my thoughts. I wrote the picture, expecting this would be a chapter in the center of the story. In the end, that first scene turned out to be the final chapter. Who knew?!

As a verbal processor, I usually don't know what I'm thinking until it comes out of my mouth. Similarly, sitting at my laptop, Mac(Beth), parts of the story flow as fresh to me as they will be to the reader. Because the scenes do not appear in sequence, I write the scenes formulating in my brain. Ideas that show up later frequently reveal information that fills in earlier gaps. "No wonder the bad guy behaves in that way." When the manuscript is nearly complete, I rearrange chapters as needed for the story to make sense, add transitions, and fill in details.

Linear

Estee Zandee writes her novels sequentially from beginning to end. Taking a break once, she returned to her manuscript to discover "what the bad guy was doing while I was away." Her natural creative process is more linear.

Hybrids

Some projects organically require an author to employ a different method than their natural go-to. There is no right or wrong way to plot a story. Write your plot using the method that works for you to get the story done, or using the method the project requires to be accurate, believable, and complete.

Chapter Ten

Thank You

T hank you for reading *Creative Characters* by P.S. Wells (PeggySue Wells) in the Quick Guide to Writing Well series *Creative Characters* is available in ebook and paperback.

If you have a moment, please leave a review on your favorite bookseller website. Reviews are the best gift you give an author.

Titles you may like by P.S. Wells include:

Quick Guides to Writing Well series
Pivotal Plots
Sensational Settings
Creative Characters
Dynamic Dialog
Point of View

Marc Wayne Adventure series
Chasing Sunrise

Check out the audio version of *Chasing Sunrise* read by Scott Hoke

The Patent

Secrecy Order

Unnatural Cause

Homeless for the Holidays

Check out the audio version of *Homeless for the Holidays* read by voice actor Katie Leigh

Personal Growth titles

The Ten Best Decisions A Single Mom Can Make

Slavery in the Land of the Free

The Girl Who Wore Freedom

C heck out these titles by PS Wells and PeggySue Wells

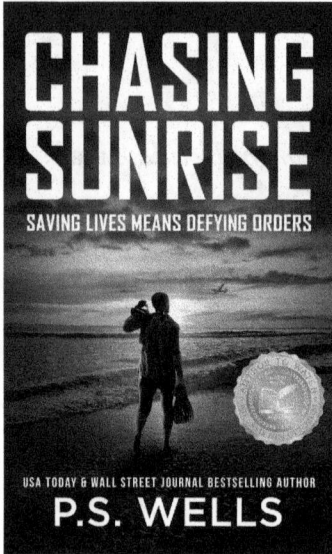

When an assignment results in a friend's death, Michael Northington seeks solace on St. Croix. When deadly players blow into St. Croix at the same time Hurricane Hugo unleashes its fury, will Michael's skills be enough to protect those he loves?

Also available in audio version, narrated by Scott Hoke.

When the world teeters on the verge of World War III, the nation that develops a patent attorney's invention will be militarily invincible in the race for global dominance. Now America's enemies have stolen the plans and kidnapped the inventor. Marc Wayne must find a way of escape before his captors realize the invention is theoretical. Or is it?

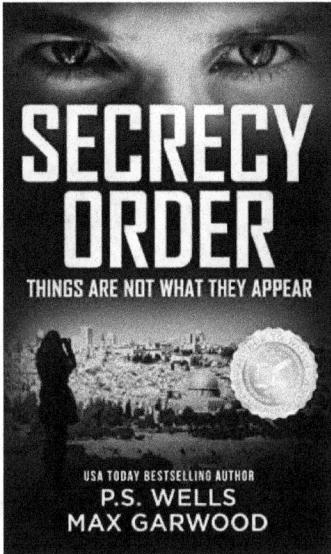

Powerful nations hunt for Marc Wayne and his invention which promises to redefine weapons and global warfare. Meanwhile, in a remote hiding place, Marc serves as bait in hopes to turn his predators into prey. When an illegal arms dealer leverages Marc for his own ends, will Marc ever see home and family again? As time runs out, can he trust the electro-physicist, Lei Quong, enough to escape with her?

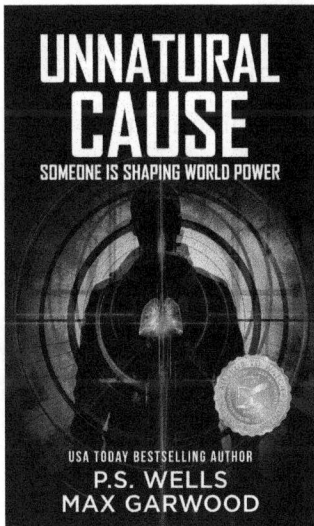

Winner of the best mystery suspense of the year, *Unnatural Cause* unpacks long unsolved family mysteries. Using a device that creates a deadly embolism from a remote location, someone is targeting world leaders to shape world power. But when Marc Wayne stops those who wield the ability to commit consequence-free murder, he finds he has played right into the mastermind's plans.

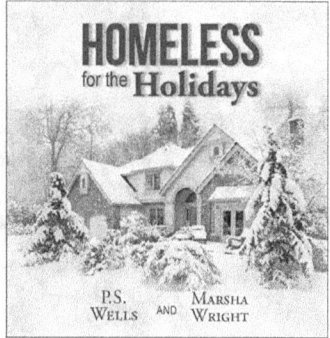

Christmas is coming, and Jack Baker's finances, friends, and future are as gone as last year's holiday. Amidst the holiday traditions and trappings, one family learns what is truly important when they lose all they have, and find they still have everything.

Also available in audio version read by voice actor Katie Leigh.

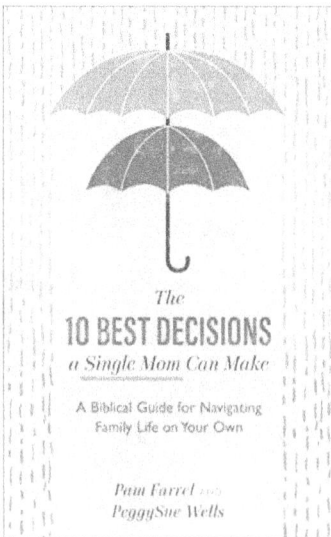

No matter how you became a single mom, you share the same challenges and fears all single moms have. How are you going to do this on your own? With humor, and sage advice, PeggySue Wells (single parent of seven children) provides practical helps and tangible tips to help you succeed.

A clear picture of how human trafficking happens and how prevalent it is today. We ended slavery once before in the United States, and we can do it again.

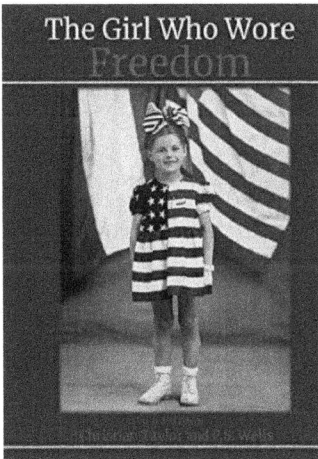

On June 6, 1944, when Dany was five years old, U.S. soldiers liberated her village from Nazi control. Soldiers established a base on Utah Beach near Dany's home, shared their provisions, and befriended the people of Sainte Marie du Mont. From the parachutes of the American soldiers who freed her, Dany's mother sewed a red, white, and blue dress resembling the American flag. Dany wore the dress at the yearly D-Day celebration and became known as *The Girl Who Wore Freedom*.

PeggySue's Particulars
to Pen

POINT OF VVIEW

A Quick Guide to
Writing Well

PEGGYSUE WELLS

You want to write and write well. Point of view is the writer's most powerful tool to elicit emotion in the reader. POV can make the difference between a character appearing as a killer or a king. Learn how to pen the proper POV that compels a reader to turn pages until reaching the end.

You want to write and write well. Use this quick guide to amplify, intensify, and magnify through plot to craft a compelling story.

In this quick how-to guide, learn the particulars to craft pivotal plots that create compelling stories.

PeggySue's Particulars
to Pen

PIVOTAL PLOTS

A Quick Guide To
Writing Well

PEGGYSUE WELLS

PeggySue's Particulars
to Pen

CREATIVE
CHARACTERS

A Quick Guide To
Writing Well

PEGGYSUE WELLS

You want to write and write well. Use this quick guide to craft creative characters that live in the reader's mind beyond the final page of a story.

Three essentials are common to every compelling story.

1) a character the reader cares about

2) a very great life-changing, world-impacting need the character must achieve

3) a great obstacle between the character we care about and the character's life-changing, world-impacting need.

In Creative Characters, learn how to craft characters who are believable, three-dimensional, and remain in the reader's memory long after the book is read.

Stories happen in a place and that place is the setting. Settings come in four personalities.

The personalities types of setting are

- Passive

- Active

- Like a Character

- Is the Story

PeggySue's Particulars
to Pen

SENSATIONAL SETTINGS

A Quick Guide To
Writing Well

PEGGYSUE WELLS

What does the setting sound like, feel like, and look like? If you plan to write a book or want to improve a story, place the tale in a sensational setting. Sensational Settings: A Quick Guide to Writing Well shows you how.

PeggySue's Particulars
to Pen

**DYNAMIC
DIALOG**

A Quick Guide To
Writing Well

PEGGYSUE WELLS

Dialog is what characters say. Powerful stories are dialog-driven through carefully chosen word selections. The four purposes of dialog in your story include:

1. Move your story forward

2. Reveal something important about your plot

3. Show something important about your character

4. Give your character a unique voice

Conversations that take place between characters are often the reader's favorite part. Add value to your story by writing dialog that is clever, creative, and concise.

About the Author

P.S. Wells is a USA Today and Wall Street Journal bestselling author of 40 books (so far). When not writing, Wells rides horses, parasails, scuba dives, and skydives. She is the founder of SingleMomCircle.com

Connect with P.S. Wells at PeggySueWells.com

www.ingramcontent.com/pod-product-compliance
Lightning Source LLC
Chambersburg PA
CBHW060524280326
41933CB00014B/3098

* 9 7 9 8 9 9 2 1 0 4 4 1 7 *